Ten Po
about Sheep

ex libris

Candlestick Press

Published by:
Candlestick Press,
Diversity House, 72 Nottingham Road,
Arnold, Nottingham NG5 6LF
www.candlestickpress.co.uk

Design, typesetting, print and production by Diversity Creative
Marketing Solutions Ltd., www.diversitymarketing.co.uk

Introduction and selection of poems © Neil Astley, 2012

Cover illustration © Beth Krommes, 2012

ISBN: 978 1 907598 11 1

Acknowledgements:
Our thanks to David Scott and Bloodaxe Books for permission to
reprint 'Flanking Sheep in Mosedale' from *Selected Poems* (Bloodaxe
Books, 1998). 'February 17th', 'Sheep' and 'Bringing in new couples'
are taken from *Collected Poems* © Estate of Ted Hughes and reprinted
by permission of Faber and Faber Ltd. Our thanks to Josephine
Dickinson and The Rialto for permission to reprint 'November',
a version of which was first published in *Scarberry Hill* (The Rialto,
2001); to Ruth Bidgood and Seren Books for permission to reprint
'Sheep in the Hedge' from *New and Selected Poems* (Seren, 2004);
to Gillian Clarke and Carcanet Press for permission to reprint 'A
Difficult Birth, Easter 1998' from *Five Fields* (Carcanet Press, 1998);
and to Jo Shapcott and Faber & Faber for permission to reprint 'Lies'
and 'Love Song with a Flock of Sheep' from *Her Book: Poems
1988 – 1998* (Faber & Faber, 2000).

Where poets are no longer living, their dates are given.

Foreword

I think my sheep obsession must go back to childhood. I cannot remember a time when I was not fascinated with sheep, and for the past twenty years I have lived in parts of Northumberland where there are more sheep than people. My adult bonding with cats and dogs made me realise I could no more eat the flesh of a sheep than I could that of a cat, dog or even a human: we are all individual beings with souls and personalities. I have to reconcile this with the knowledge that sheep wouldn't exist without the horribly named sheep industry, nor would I be able to indulge in sheep-watching if someone else weren't raising sheep for other humans to eat.

I live next to a field with a motley flock of mostly Scottish blackface ewes, which comes alive with squealing, joyful lambs every spring. Summer brings the short trauma of shearing. A few months later their young are taken away. After two or three days of loud protest at their loss, the uncomprehending mothers return to the business of tearing up and munching the grass. Life goes on. Come autumn, the eager tups are let into the field and quickly sample all the talent. Ewes without the tup's telltale raddle mark on their rump will go for slaughter; likewise the flagging tup who doesn't meet his target. Mutton, both. There's no room for slack. The hill farmer's year-long care and costs are his investment. His business only shows the profit he needs to survive if enough healthy lambs go for slaughter. Yet this life drama of the cared-for victim animal has rarely attracted the interest of poets.

For all that English literature has a centuries-old pastoral tradition, very few poets actually write about sheep, the beasts themselves who live out their short lives so we can fleece them of their flesh and wool. John Clare's *Shepherd's Calendar* charts the lives of shepherds, not sheep. Wordsworth was more inspired by shepherds ('The Last of the Flock') and shepherdesses ('The Pet Lamb') than by Lakeland sheep.

William Blake turned his innocent 'Lamb' into a religious symbol of sacrifice. R.S. Thomas may have written a poem called 'Looking at Sheep', but its subject isn't sheep but Welsh nationalism, while Sylvia Plath's 'Sheep in Fog' fathoms her own psychological crisis. Even the 'Ettrick Shepherd' James Hogg's best writing was concerned not with sheep but with the sins of mankind.

Perhaps not surprisingly the most authentic and brilliantly observed poetry about sheep has been written by poets who have lived and worked with the animals, most notably Ted Hughes, who raised sheep and cattle on a farm in Devon for many years. Gillian Clarke in Wales and Josephine Dickinson in Cumbria have likewise combined poem-writing with sheep-rearing. All three writers have produced many more poems about sheep than I have been able to represent in a gathering which has to include other excellent varieties of sheep poems.

I do hope that these ten poems about sheep will give readers a greater understanding and sympathy for a poorly understood and too often maligned animal. Sheep may not be as intelligent as humans, or pigs (their IQ is rated as on par with that of cows), but when we talk of people behaving like sheep, what we actually mean is that they don't think for themselves in following the lead of other humans. Sheep, however, are gregarious animals unable to defend themselves from predators or humans, and a flock instinctively follows its leader to new pastures. Sheep behaviour assists survival, whereas human herd behaviour is unthinking, undermining and courts disaster. It is surely time we celebrated sheep for being sheep and for behaving like sheep, even when held captive by carnivorous humans. These ten excellent poems do just that.

Neil Astley

The Lambs of Grasmere, 1860

The upland flocks grew starved and thinned:
    Their shepherds scarce could feed the lambs
Whose milkless mothers butted them,
    Or who were orphaned of their dams.
The lambs athirst for mother's milk
    Filled all the place with piteous sounds:
Their mothers' bones made white for miles
    The pastureless wet pasture grounds.

Day after day, night after night,
    From lamb to lamb the shepherds went,
With teapots for the bleating mouths
    Instead of nature's nourishment.
The little shivering gaping things
    Soon knew the step that brought them aid,
And fondled the protecting hand,
    And rubbed it with a woolly head.

Then, as the days waxed on to weeks,
    It was a pretty sight to see
These lambs with frisky heads and tails
    Skipping and leaping on the lea,
Bleating in tender, trustful tones,
    Resting on rocky crag or mound,
And following the beloved feet
    That once had sought for them and found.

These very shepherds of their flocks,
   These loving lambs so meek to please,
Are worthy of recording words
   And honour in their due degrees:
So I might live a hundred years,
   And roam from strand to foreign strand,
Yet not forget this flooded spring
   And scarce-saved lambs of Westmoreland.

Christina Rossetti (1830 – 1894)

Flanking Sheep in Mosedale

All summer the sheep were strewn like crumbs
across the fell, until the bracken turned brittle
and it was time they were gathered
into the green patchwork of closer fields.
Dogs and men sweep a whole hillside in minutes
save for the stray, scared into a scramble
up a gully. A dog is detached: whistled off
by the shepherd who in one hand
holds a pup straining at the baling twine
and in the other, a crook light as a baton.
His call cuts the wind across the tarn:
it is the voice of the first man, who
booted it across this patch to bring
strays to the place where he would have them.
You can tell that here is neither love nor money
but the old game fathers have taught sons to win.
It is done well, when the dogs
lie panting, and the sheep encircled dare not move.

David Scott

February 17th

A lamb could not get born. Ice wind
Out of a downpour dishclout sunrise. The mother
Lay on the mudded slope. Harried, she got up
And the blackish lump bobbed at her back-end
Under her tail. After some hard galloping,
Some manoeuvring, much flapping of the backward
Lump head of the lamb looking out,
I caught her with a rope. Laid her, head uphill
And examined the lamb. A blood-ball swollen
Tight in its black felt, its mouth gap
Squashed crooked, tongue stuck out, black-purple,
Strangled by its mother. I felt inside,
Past the noose of mother-flesh, into the slippery
Muscled tunnel, fingering for a hoof,
Right back to the port-hole of the pelvis.
But there was no hoof. He had stuck his head out too early
And his feet could not follow. He should have
Felt his way, tip-toe, his toes
Tucked up under his nose
For a safe landing. So I kneeled wrestling
With her groans. No hand could squeeze past
The lamb's neck into her interior
To hook a knee. I roped that baby head
And hauled till she cried out and tried
To get up and I saw it was useless. I went
Two miles for the injection and a razor.
Sliced the lamb's throat-strings, levered with a knife
Between the vertebrae and brought the head off
To stare at its mother, its pipes sitting in the mud
With all earth for a body. Then pushed
The neck-stump right back in, and as I pushed
She pushed. She pushed crying and I pushed gasping.

And the strength
Of the birth push and the push of my thumb
Against that wobbly vertebra were deadlock,
A to-fro futility. Till I forced
A hand past and got a knee. Then like
Pulling myself to the ceiling with one finger
Hooked in a loop, timing my effort
To her birth push groans, I pulled against
The corpse that would not come. Till it came.
And after it the long, sudden, yolk-yellow
Parcel of life
In a smoking slither of oils and soups and syrups –
And the body lay born, beside the hacked-off head.

17 February 1974

Ted Hughes (1930 – 1998)

Sheep

I

The sheep has stopped crying.
All morning in her wire-mesh compound
On the lawn, she has been crying
For her vanished lamb. Yesterday they came.
Then her lamb could stand, in a fashion,
And make some tiptoe cringing steps.
Now he has disappeared.
He was only half the proper size,
And his cry was wrong. It was not
A dry little hard bleat, a baby-cry
Over a flat tongue, it was human,
It was a despairing human smooth Oh!
Like no lamb I ever heard. Its hindlegs
Cowered in under its lumped spine,
Its feeble hips leaned towards
Its shoulders for support. Its stubby
White wool pyramid head, on a tottery neck,
Had sad and defeated eyes, pinched, pathetic,
Too small, and it cried all the time
Oh! Oh! staggering towards
Its alert, baffled, stamping, storming mother
Who feared our intentions. He was too weak
To find her teats, or to nuzzle up in under,
He hadn't the gumption. He was fully
Occupied just standing, then shuffling
Towards where she'd removed to. She knew
He wasn't right, she couldn't
Make him out. Then his rough-curl legs,
So stoutly built, and hooved
With real quality tips,
Just got in the way, like a loose bundle
Of firewood he was cursed to manage,
Too heavy for him, lending sometimes
Some support, but no strength, no real help.

When we sat his mother on her tail, he mouthed her teat,
Slobbered a little, but after a minute
Lost aim and interest, his muzzle wandered,
He was managing a difficulty
Much more urgent and important. By evening
He could not stand. It was not
That he could not thrive, he was born
With everything but the will –
That can be deformed, just like a limb.
Death was more interesting to him.
Life could not get his attention.
So he died, with the yellow birth-mucus
Still in his cardigan.
He did not survive a warm summer night.
Now his mother has started crying again.
The wind is oceanic in the elms
And the blossom is all set.

II

What is it this time the dark barn again
Where men jerk me off my feet
And shout over me with murder voices
And do something painful to somewhere on my body

Why am I grabbed by the leg and dragged from my friends
Where I was hidden safe though it was hot
Why am I dragged into the light and whirled onto my back
Why am I sat up on my rear end with my legs splayed

A man grips me helpless his knees grip me helpless
What is that buzzer what is it coming
Buzzing like a big fierce insect on a long tangling of snake
What is the man doing to me with his buzzing thing

That I cannot see he is pressing it into me
I surrender I let my legs kick I let myself be killed

I let him hoist me about he twists me flat
In a leverage of arms and legs my neck pinned under his ankle

While he does something dreadful down the whole length of my
 belly
My little teats stand helpless and terrified as he buzzes around
 them

Poor old ewe! She peers around from her ridiculous position.
Cool intelligent eyes, of grey-banded agate and amber,

Eyes deep and clear with feeling and understanding
While her monster hooves dangle helpless
And a groan like no bleat vibrates in her squashed windpipe
And the cutter buzzes at her groin and her fleece piles away

Now it buzzes at her throat and she emerges whitely
More and more grotesquely female and nude
Paunchy and skinny, while her old rug, with its foul tassels
Heaps from her as a foam-stiff, foam-soft, yoke-yellow robe

Numbed all over she suddenly feels much lighter
She feels herself free, her legs are her own and she scrambles up
Waiting for that grapple of hands to fling her down again
She stands in the opened arch of his knees she is facing a
 bright doorway

With a real bleat to comfort the lamb in herself
She trots across the threshold and makes one high clearing
 bound
To break from the cramp of her fright
And surprised by her new lightness and delighted

She trots away, noble-nosed, her pride unsmirched.
Her greasy winter-weight stays coiled on the foul floor, for
 somebody else to bother about.
She has a beautiful wet green brand on her bobbing brand-new
 backside,
She baas, she has come off best.

III

The mothers have come back
From the shearing, and behind the hedge
The woe of sheep is like a battlefield
In the evening, when the fighting is over,
And the cold begins, and the dew falls,
And bowed women move with water.
Mother mother mother the lambs
Are crying, and the mothers are crying.
Nothing can resist that probe, that cry
Of a lamb for its mother, or an ewe's crying
For its lamb. The lambs cannot find
Their mothers among those shorn strangers.
A half-hour they have lamented,
Shaking their voices in desperation.
Bald brutal-voiced mothers braying out,
Flat-tongued lambs chopping off hopelessness,
Their hearts are in panic, their bodies
Are a mess of woe, woe they cry,
They mingle their trouble, a music
Of worse and worse distress, a worse entangling,
They hurry out little notes
With all their strength, cries searching this way and that.
The mothers force out sudden despair, blaaa!
On restless feet, with wild heads.

Their anguish goes on and on, in the June heat.
Only slowly their hurt dies, cry by cry,
As they fit themselves to what has happened.

Ted Hughes (1930 – 1998)

Bringing in new couples

Wind out of freezing Europe. A mean snow
Fiery cold. Ewes caked crusty with snow,
Their new hot lambs wet trembling
And crying on trampled patches, under the hedge –
Twenty miles of open lower landscape
Blows into their wetness. The field smokes and writhes
Burning like a moor with snow-fumes.
Lambs nestling to make themselves comfortable
While the ewe nudges and nibbles at them
And the numbing snow-wind blows on the blood tatters
At her breached back-end.
The moor a grey sea-shape. The wood
Thick-fingered density, a worked wall of whiteness.
The old sea-roar, sheep-shout, lamb-wail.
Redwings needling invisible. A fright
Smoking among trees, the hedges blocked.
Lifting of ice-heavy ewes, trampling anxieties
As they follow their wide-legged tall lambs,
Tripods craning to cry bewildered.
We coax the mothers to follow their babies
And they do follow, running back
In sudden convinced panic to the patch
Where the lamb had been born, dreading
She must have been deceived away from it
By crafty wolvish humans, then coming again
Defenceless to the bleat she's attuned to
And recognizing her own – a familiar
Detail in the meaningless shape-mass
Of human arms, legs, body-clothes – her lamb on the white earth
Held by those hands. Then vanishing again
Lifted. Then only the disembodied cry
Going with the human, while she runs in a circle
On the leash of the cry. While the wind
Presses outer space into the grass

And alarms wrens deep in brambles
With hissing fragments of stars.

16 February 1975

Ted Hughes (1930 – 1998)

A Difficult Birth, Easter 1998

An old ewe that somehow till this year
had given the ram the slip. We thought her barren.
Good Friday, and the Irish peace deal close,
and tonight she's serious, restless and hoofing the straw.
We put off the quiet supper and bottle of wine
we'd planned, to celebrate if the news is good.

Her waters broke an hour ago and she's sipped
her own lost salty ocean from the ground.
While they slog it out in Belfast, eight decades
since Easter 1916, exhausted, tamed by pain,
she licks my fingers with a burning tongue,
lies down again. Two hooves and a muzzle.

But the lamb won't come. You phone for help
and step into the lane to watch for car lights.
This is when the whitecoats come to the women,
well-meaning, knowing best, with their needles and forceps.
So I ease my fingers in, take the slippery head
in my right hand, two hooves in my left.

We strain together, harder than we dared.
I feel a creak in the limbs and pull till he comes
in a syrupy flood. She drinks him, famished, and you find us
peaceful, at a cradling that might have been a death.
Then the second lamb slips through her opened door,
the stone rolled away.

Gillian Clarke

November

He trots in every morning
with the fluorescent mark
on his back. The first couple
of times, it was tentative,
after he'd fed with the ewes,
but now he appears by the
gate at the start of feeding
time. He gets plenty of maize
as well as black nuts, which
is what he likes. The hens go
bananas. There's always more
than enough both for him and
for them. He is so tiny
he doesn't look as if he'll
ever fatten up. He stands
apart always from the ewes,
even from his twin sister.
He cannot understand where
the three other wethers have
gone (they went to market in
Carlisle last week). He comes in
every morning full of hope
for his morning feed. One day
he will come in and be killed.
Will he know when that's to be?
Marra, do you know when you
too will die, or even how?

Josephine Dickinson

Sheep in the Hedge

This is no mild and never-never sheep
but a heavy wild thing, mad with fright,
catapulting at you from a noose of brambles,
hurtling back into worse frenzy of tangles.
Don't imagine you are welcome.
Don't expect gratitude.
That woolly maniac would hate you
if she had any consciousness to spare
from panic. She can see sideways.
There is too much world forcing itself
through slit eyes into her dim brain –
a spiky overpowering pattern of thorns.
Now, worst of all, she suffers the sight of you
(no doubt malevolent), hideously near,
touching her! She wrenches, rips, breaks out,
knocks you into the hedge and is away,
her plump bedraggled body jogging down the road
full-pelt on sticks of legs, pert hooves. You are left
to mop your dripping scratches and stitch up
the tatters of your good intentions.

Ruth Bidgood

Lies

In reality, sheep are brave, enlightened
and sassy. They are walking clouds
and like clouds have forgotten
how to jump. As lambs they knew.
Lambs jump because in their innocence
they still find grass exciting.
Some turf is better for tiptoeing
say the lambs. Springy meadows
have curves which invite fits
of bouncing and heel-kicking
to turn flocks of lambs
into demented white spuds boiling in the pot.
Then there is a French style of being a lamb
which involves show and a special touch
at angling the bucking legs. Watch carefully
next time: Lambs love to demonstrate –
you won't have to inveigle.
Eventually, of course, lambs grow trousers
and a blast of wool
which keeps them anchored to the sward.
Then grass is first and foremost
savoury, not palpable.
I prefer the grown sheep: even when damp
she is brave, enlightened and sassy,
her eye a kaleidoscope of hail and farewell,
her tail her most eloquent organ of gesture.
When she speaks, it is to tell me
that she is under a spell, polluted.
Her footwear has been stolen
and the earth rots her feet.
In reality she walks across the sky
upside-down in special pumps.

Jo Shapcott

Love Song with a Flock of Sheep

'Win a flock of sheep' said the advertisement.
'Sheep Dip: an eight year old pure malt whisky.
You will find an entry form on every bottle.'

I will. I will buy the whisky,
I will find the entry form. I will:
I will win the sheep and I'll give them to you.

Keep the flock at home
and let them graze around the house.
Kindly and damp, they'll eat the carpet
and will start on the wallpaper too;
your interior decorations will be masticated away.
The flock is softer than soft furnishings
but when they've eaten all that they'll start
on the hard stuff. They'll munch their way
through the mantelpiece and everything –
your books, your manuscripts –
will fly into their placid mouths.

I know you. You'll like it better without
all that ruminated stuff. You want
the woolly life, carding and spinning,
with only sheep for furniture and bedclothes.
The flock will find you out eventually
and start their blowing in your ears
and their nuzzling across your hair.
It will begin in the kitchen with a fleecy
brush along the backs of your knees.

They'll surround you on the sofa
and drink out of your bath. Your clothes
will go into the three stomachs and in the dark
you'll feel sheep nibble between your toes
and suck your toenails. They will graze
your legs, removing every hair with teeth
so precise and shy you'll feel only
a mist of breath and lips. They'll move
in a cloud across your chest, your belly,
face and beard – everywhere – cropped
down to a downy stubble, peaceful as pasture.
Soon you will be as shorn as a yearling lamb
and twice as happy, blissoming with the flock.

When I arrive, dressed as Bo-Peep,
I won't get a look in. But by hook or by crook
you shall have them anyway: sheep fleecy, sheep shorn
and me lovelorn.

Jo Shapcott

Dear Shawn

Happy Birthday

All our love

Patrick + Maria
X X
                        X X